GOLF GAMES

Golf Trip Junkie's Favorite Wagering Games

GOLF TRIP JUNKIE

GOLF GAMES

ISBN-13: 978-1503078031
ISBN-10: 1503078035

...uber awesome golf holidays.

GOLF

TRIP JUNKIE

WWW.GOLFTRIPJUNKIE.COM

Table of Contents

SECTION 3: Golf Games for 4 Players

SECTION 4: Golf Games for Larger Groups

SECTION 5: Side Games

If your opponent is playing several shots in vain attempts to extricate himself from a bunker, do not stand near him and audibly count his strokes. It would be justifiable homicide if he wound up his pitiable exhibition by applying his niblick to your head.

—Harry Vardon

A Personal Message

Over the years, I have enjoyed numerous golf trips with friends of mine. Inevitably, either during the planning phase of the trip OR on the way to the airport OR while having a cold beverage (or two) when we arrive at the hotel, the following question is asked:

"What game are we playing?"

As you can imagine, the discussion erupts, taking on a life of its own, as four grown men try to figure out the best way to *rob each other blind* during the upcoming rounds of golf.

As comical as those discussions are—often not only isolated to golf vacations—we simply enjoy the pursuit of intrigue and challenge in our rounds of golf. We want to feel some pressure, see what all the *fuss* is about with sweaty palms, knees quivering, and an amplified heart rate as we're faced with a 3-foot putt for par . . . A putt that, with minimal effort, we can *normally* tap in on any given Sunday.

With wagers comes laughter . . .

You know what I mean . . . You're watching your good

pal Johnny as he is sweating over a 3-footer for par, knowing full well he rarely misses BUT *hoping* like hell he does. The *hoping* is far greater than the desire to win the $5 Nassau. In fact, that $5 or $25 really doesn't matter much one way or another, because being the person you are, you will likely buy the first round of drinks with your winnings anyway. Admit it, you will . . . and you like doing it too!

Instead, the *hoping* Johnny misses the putt all comes back to what golf is supposed to be about for us weekend choppers (If we're not playing college golf, on mini-tours, or the PGA Tour, we're choppers . . . All of us!) and that's having a good chuckle. A little laugh at our buddy's expense as the sure-to-be ensuing reaction of his missed putt will be nothing short of comical.

Likely, laugh-out-loud-slap-your-knee hysterical as Johnny's reaction resembles that of doomsday or the Master's was just lost . . . Or both!

You see . . . golf is supposed to be fun. More importantly, the fun should bring out the best of friendships and relationships, bringing people closer together, even if during those times you're not too fond of your *so-called friends* as they are having a laugh on your behalf.

That lack of fondness eventually fades.

And from it, lasting memories evolve.

As the Founder and CEO of Golf Trip Junkie, I decided to write, self-publish, and give my customers a copy of *Golf Games: Golf Trip Junkie's Favorite Wagering Games* as added value to their memorable golf trips booked through my company. Of course, anyone else picking up a copy of *Golf Games* through Amazon (or elsewhere) will also be able to spice up the entertainment value with their buddies or significant other during their Saturday morning games.

Warning!

Golf Games: Golf Trip Junkie's Favorite Wagering Games is by no means the full gamut of all golf games that have been created and wagered upon countless times since the beginning of time. No Sir. No Ma'am. I'll get that out of the way right from the start (Just in case there are any naysayers!).

Quite honestly, I hate to think about how long such an endeavor—*write, edit, write some more, then edit some more, "Oh crap, I missed a game!", write some more, edit some more, then finally publish*—would take. Instead, I wanted to serve my customers and readers with an action-packed, fun-filled, and simple sample size handbook of some of my favorite golf games. In turn, perhaps in time, they will also be some of your favorites as well. Besides, isn't golf complicated enough that a 200-page book of golf games is overkill?

Many golfers shy away from golf games . . .

Another *method to my madness* is that many golfers—not

all—tend to stay away from golf games because they are either too afraid of *losing their shirt* or the games can be too darn confusing . . . Or both! So why complicate matters? Simple, fun, and easy to use works best, don't you think?

In *Golf Games*, you will find many different games for varying group sizes. More importantly, however, they are games for all playing abilities. My hope for you is that it keeps everyone involved and having some fun—especially while on vacation—even when your game isn't going as well as planned.

So that's my story, and I'm stickin' to it.

I sincerely hope you enjoy *Golf Games: Golf Trip Junkie's Favorite Wagering Games*!

Now, what are you waiting for? Turn the page and learn how to best utilize the book I have created for you.

And of course . . . Thank You!

Sean Petersen
Founder & CEO
Golf Trip Junkie
WWW.GOLFTRIPJUNKIE.COM

How to Use *Golf Games*

For your convenience, *Golf Games* is outlined in the following way:

Section 1: Golf Games for 2 Players
Section 2: Golf Games for 3 Players
Section 3: Golf Games for 4 Players
Section 4: Golf Games for Larger Groups
Section 5: Side Games

The games are placed under the sections that I think are most ideal for that group size. Of course, many games are just as ideal for other group sizes. In those instances, I made the navigation easy for you. For example, at the end of *Section 2: Golf Games for 3 Players*, you will see other games for threesomes, and where to find them.

You will also find an *Index of Golf Games* at the end of *Golf Games*. This index shows the page numbers for each game, as well as the number of players each game is considered ideal for.

User-friendly . . . I hope.
Happy golfing!

SECTION 1

Golf Games for 2 Players

Bisque

Do you have a golf hole that gives you fits?

Or . . . Scorecard in hand, are you moments away from teeing off on the first round of your buddy's golf trip, and despite what the hole-by-hole handicap ratings say, there are a couple holes that keep popping out, grabbing your attention . . . destined to give you nightmares? (Let's be honest . . . We all know what this feels like, however, some are more honest than others!).

If so, then *Bisque* is ideal you.

For the folks that know what I'm talking about, here is the rundown of *Bisque* . . .

Instead of using the scorecard handicap for each hole, a player can determine *when* and *where* they are going to use their handicap.

Of course, this declaration has to be made before launching their tee shot. It seems rather obvious to say, but not everyone is like me where they announce to their group "Under no certain terms am I hitting *that* ball out of *that* bunker!"

When playing *Bisque*, remember, there is a maximum of two strokes to be used on the hole. If you need more than two strokes on a hole, perhaps—maybe, just maybe—you're on the wrong kind of trip. Perhaps buying a boat in the near future is a good idea? Or taking a cruise instead?

Kidding of course. Or am I?

Bisque can also be played with groups of three or four players, as well as in larger groups.

Three Little Pigs

Never hear of *Three Little Pigs*? Well, you're in for a treat.

Three Little Pigs is an ideal golf game for players of any skill level. In fact, the golfers on your golf trip that should have considered investing in a boat years ago are going to love this game!

Here's how *Three Little Pigs* works . . .

Upon completion of your round, when all that's left are the tears and enjoying a cold beverage of your choice, each player strikes three scores from their score, totaling up the remaining 15 scores for their final score.

Three Little Pigs allows for each player to have the occasional big number or blow up in a round, giving them some hope to remain competitive in the game.

This game can be played as singles or as partners in best-ball or net best-ball . . . Essentially in many of the games where you keep score.

Three Little Pigs can also be played with three or four players, as well as in larger groups.

Three Blind Mice

In *Three Blind Mice*, follow the rules of *Three Little Pigs*, doing everything as you normally would, however, upon completion of your round make your way to the lounge for your beverage and do one of the following:

1. Ask a server to pick three random numbers between 1 and 18 OR . . .
2. Grab a napkin, write 1 through 18 on it, then break each number into the 18 selections that go into a hat for a draw.

Of course, the easiest way is to ask your server to pick three numbers.

Once those three numbers are selected, go through the scores and eliminate those selected holes from the scorecard for each player, totaling up the remaining 15 holes, which is now your score.

Settle the bets, and watch closely as the guy that didn't have any big numbers or any blow ups *sulk* because of bad luck as they lose.

Three Blind Mice can also be played in groups of three, four, or more players.

Snake

Nobody likes slow play. Heck, even slow players don't like slow play. Go figure.

Why state the obvious in this chapter on *Snake*?

If at all possible, *Snake* is a game best played when the course is a little less crowded. However, if you are in the middle of a traffic jam, then have a go with *Snake*.

Here's how *Snake* works . . .

Instead of swatting away *gimme* putts, *Snake* forces golfers to putt-out at all times.

Set an agreed amount for the wager at the beginning of the round. This agreed amount is added to the *pot of gold* every time a golfer 3-putts—the ball has to be on the green for the first putt . . . Second putt, not so much!

The last person to 3-putt in the round is the *loser*, the unfortunate one to have to pay each player the amount in the pot.

There are other modified versions of *Snake*, one of which includes more progressive deposits into the pot. The first 3-putt could be .25 cents, then double it up for each 3-putt that follows.

How much should you bet?

Well, you and your group know best. If doubling it up each time a 3-putt occurs, some players may be more comfortable with a quarter, while others may *think* they are high-rollers—"Quarters are for kids!" they might say—so nothing less than a $50-spot to start.

It's your call, as long as everyone is comfortable.

There is an added bonus to *Snake* in that it puts some of the stress and pressure back into those little 3-foot putts. Hopefully it will make you a better putter.

No harm in hoping . . .

Snake can also be played in groups of three or four players, as well as a side game.

Mutt and Jeff

In *Mutt and Jeff*, the focus of the scoring is on par-3's and par-5's only.

The scoring system is rather simple, so no worries about stressing yourself out by trying to figure this game out.

At the end of your round, the players tally up their par-3 and par-5 scores, which is now their *total score* for the round.

The lowest score wins the predetermined wager, which was set before getting the first tee shot airborne.

You can play *Mutt and Jeff* in straight up stroke play or you can use handicaps to get the total net score, making it ideal for all levels of golfers.

Mutt and Jeff can also be played in groups of three or four players, as well as in larger groups of players. You can also consider playing *Mutt and Jeff* as a side game within your game.

Nassau

Nassau is very likely the best-known and most popular golf game amongst golfers. You will also know you're playing *Nassau* when someone says "You wanna go 5-5-5?" (a $5 Nassau, as an example).

Here's how it works:

- ✓ Designate a dollar amount, normally a $1 or a $2 or a $5 Nassau.
- ✓ Each Nassau applies to the front nine, the back nine, and long-game (full round).
- ✓ The winner of each Nassau is the golfer that wins the front nine, the back nine, and the long-game (typically played in match play).

If you are playing in a twosome for a $5 Nassau, for example, the most that can be lost by each player is $15.

Nassau can also be played in groups of 4 split into teams of two.

If that is not interesting enough, you can play *Nassau* with the option to *press*, *automatic 2-down press* (even have *unlimited presses*). It does require a little more focus—

and some math skills—when throwing presses around.

Each *press* (essentially *double-or-nothing*) is the same dollar value of the original bet.

To avoid confusion, the only outline of *Nassau* in this chapter will be for a $5 Nassau with an *automatic 2-down press*. If you can get the hang of scoring this way, then you will be more than fine with *regular presses* and *unlimited presses*.

So let's get started.

We have two players, Joe and Bill, playing a $5 Nassau (match play scoring) with an *automatic 2-down press*. Bill gives Joe one shot on the front nine and one shot on the back nine. For those unfamiliar with indicating stroke holes on a scorecard, simply place a little checkmark in a box, in line with a player (or team). For example, on this particular day, Joe gets a stroke on the 5th hole and the 12th hole. These holes, which rank as the first and second toughest holes, will have checkmarks in their respective boxes in line with Joe's scores.

Bill is keeping score. Any hole he wins will be indicated on the scorecard by the "+" sign. When Joe wins a hole you will place a "—" sign. A hole tied is a "/".

To indicate a new press, do so by drawing a thicker vertical "|" on the scorecard where the it begins. Make the vertical line long enough to separate all scores on the hole where each press occurs.

Now for the game:

Bill gets off to a fast start, going 1-up with an eagle on the par-5 first hole. They tie the 2nd hole, and Bill wins the 3rd hole. Joe is now 2-down, therefore, an automatic press ensues.

The press will be indicated on the scorecard by the thicker " | " dividing the 3rd and 4th hole scores. In a box on the 3rd hole, you will mark *+2* for the front nine game.

Both players tie the next hole, and they each make a score of 4 on the 5th hole, however, because Joe gets a stroke here, he wins the hole. On holes 6 thru 8, Bill turns on his game and wins each hole, to go 4-up in the front nine, and 2-up in the first press, which brings on another automatic press. Insert a thicker vertical " | " separating #8 and #9.

The markings on the 8th hole will now be *+4/+2*, as Bill is 4-up in the front nine game and 2-up in the press (In this case, the "/" separates the two games).

Bill and Joe tie the 9th hole. The scoring for the front nine is as follows:

- ❖ Front nine +4
- ❖ Press 1 +2
- ❖ Press 2 Tie
- ❖ +$10 (Bill is keeping score, therefore, +$10)

The long-game continues with Bill being 4-up.

Bill wins the 10th hole, to go 5-up in the long-game, and 1-up in the back nine.

They tie the 11th, and Joe wins 12 and 13, including

an outright win on #12 (Joe's second stroke hole). He is now 3-down in the long-game, 1-up in the back nine game.

Joe wins the 14th with a birdie, while Bill, not able to find his game, makes a double-bogey. Joe is now only 2-down in the long-game and 2-up in the back nine. There is an automatic press, the first of the back nine. The markings will read *−2.* (Remember, Bill is keeping score so he shows *−2*).

Both players tie the 15th hole, while Joe goes on another run, winning 16 and 17. He is now 4-up in the back nine game, and 2-up in the first back nine press, therefore, a second back nine press ensues (Insert thick vertical " | " between #17 and #18). The markings in a box on the 17th hole are *−4/−2.*

Joe wins the 18th hole with a long birdie putt, also winning the long-game 1-up.

The back nine finishes as follows:
- ❖ Back nine: −5
- ❖ Press 1: −3
- ❖ Press 2: −1
- ❖ −$15 (Bill is keeping score, therefore, −$15)

The Final Tally:
- ❖ Bill wins $10 from the front nine games
- ❖ Joe wins $15 from the back nine games
- ❖ Joe wins $5 from the long-game (1-up)
- ❖ Joe wins a total of $10

Simple enough, right? Don't let the scoring scare you

from playing *Nassau*. Once you get the hang of it you'll be good.

If you are interested, you can consider playing with *double presses*, where the original Nassau stays as is, but the press is double ($10 instead of $5, in this example).

Of course, you can really get going and play *unlimited presses*. If you do, simply apply the same scoring and markings to keep the games organized.

If you like the idea of *Nassau* with presses, but fear it getting a little out of hand, no problem. Have one press each nine with 4-holes remaining (or any hole on each nine).

The important thing, however, is that everyone is comfortable with the wagers and fully understands the potential (and risks) involved. If you like the idea of really testing your game with *automatic 2-down presses* or *unlimited presses*, but not a $5 Nassau, then start lower with a $1 or $2 Nassau instead.

Keep in mind that you can decline presses, but that's not cool.

Again, *Nassau* can also be played in teams of two within your group of four.

If you're really interested in confusing yourself, you can also play *Nassau* in groups of three players, each playing against one another. Hope you're organized though.

Hint: Have a couple extra scorecards handy.

Other Golf Games for 2 Players

The following games and their descriptions can be found in *Section 2, Golf Games for 3 Players*. These games are also ideal for groups of 2 players:

SECTION 2

Golf Games for 3 Players

Bingo, Bango, Bongo!

Bingo, Bango, Bongo! is all about points. Even better, you don't have to worry about Johnny sandbagging again as it's perfect for golfers of all playing ability.

Here's how *Bingo, Bango Bongo!* works . . .

The first player in the group to get their ball on the green gets the *Bingo* (first point). Next up, the player whose ball is closest to the hole, once all balls are on the green, gets the *Bango* (second point). And finally, the player in the group who is first to hole out gets the *Bongo* (third point).

Are you getting the picture so far?

Because a player only has to be the first in the group to accomplish one of the three achievements, it allows for an equal playing field. In fact, the *Bango* really helps spread the wealth amongst all skill levels. For example, better golfers are more likely to hit a higher number of greens in regulation than weaker players, however, the better player may end up with more 20-foot putts for birdie. Meanwhile, the weaker player might take five shots to get close to the green but then sneak a chip to within a few feet from the hole.

Although the *better* player(s) hit the green first, the

weaker player that finally reaches the green, yet chips it up nice and close, wins the *Bango* (assuming they are closest to the hole).

So there are no disagreements, following good golf etiquette for order of play is particularly important when playing *Bingo Bango Bongo!*. The golfer that is furthest away always plays first.

You can make it interesting by allotting triple points if a player wins all *Bingo, Bango,* and *Bongo's!* on a hole.

Bingo, Bango, Bongo! is also ideal for groups of four players, as well as for side games.

Nine Points

Nine Points is a great game for a group of three players.
Here's how *Nine Points* works . . .

There are 9 points allotted to each hole, by which
you can place a dollar value for each point. How carried
away you get with this dollar value is entirely up to you,
however, set it so everyone is comfortable.

The points are distributed as follows:

❖ The winner of a hole—lowest score—receives
5 points
❖ The second lowest score gets 3 points
❖ The highest score gets 1 point

Answers to some obvious questions:

✓ If two players tie with the lowest score, they get
4 points each while the remaining player
receives 1 point.
✓ If two players tie for the second lowest score
(highest in this case) they each receive 2 points,
while the winning score gets the 5 points.
✓ If all three players tie with the same score, they

split the 9 points with 3 each other.

Following the round of golf, enjoy a cold beverage of your choice in the lounge, and total up the points. Distribute the winnings as required.

Rabbit

The premise behind *Rabbit* is the winner of a hole, with no ties, is awarded the rabbit.

When a player wins the rabbit on a hole (no ties), they keep it until a player in the group gets the lower score (no ties) on a following hole. Once this happens, the rabbit is set free and up for grabs on the next hole. Again, the winner of that hole, without ties, is awarded the rabbit.

You can make it interesting by throwing in side bets or bonus awards for the player that has the rabbit at the end of the 9th hole and the 18th hole.

If you want to ensure that money changes hands at the end of the round, you can eliminate the *set free* component of the game. Instead of the rabbit being back up for grabs after a victorious hole, it now changes hands immediately when a player has the lowest score (no ties).

The point system used can be based on the number of times a player had the rabbit. Following the round, total it up, plus any bonus points you have, and pay up accordingly.

Rabbit is also ideal for groups of four players.

Defender

Defender is a betting game, whereby, on each hole, a player is designated as the Defender.

At the beginning of the round, determine the rotation of the Defender, so it plays out in that sequence for the entire round of golf.

The points are awarded as follows:

- ✓ When the Defender wins the hole, they are awarded with 3 points while the other three players lose 1 point each.
- ✓ When the Defender loses the hole, they lose 3 points while the other players get 1 point each.
- ✓ When the Defender ties the hole, that player gets 1.5 points while the other three players lose a half point each.

As with most games, the game can be played for points, with a dollar figure per point agreed upon at the beginning of each round.

Skins

In *Skins*, the group determines whether each hole is worth a certain point or a specific dollar amount. This is done at the beginning of each round. Once agreed upon, each player throws the predetermined dollar amount into the pot before the first tee shot is launched.

The round is played out as follows . . .

The player with the lowest score on a hole wins the skin. However, if two or more players tie, the skin is carried over to the next hole. A hole (skin) can only be won when there is an outright winner.

Continue the process throughout the entire round, until the last putt drops.

The money owing is settled based on the agreed point system or dollar amount from the beginning of the round.

A modified way of playing *Skins* is in larger groups, whereby players throw a predetermined dollar amount into the pot at the beginning of the round. One player in each group keeps score, and at the end of the round the group gathers with the scorecards, scanning each hole for an outright winner of a hole.

If there is an outright winner for a hole, that player wins a skin, getting a portion of the pot. So if there are four skins won, and the pot is $1000, each winning player would receive $250.

Skins can also be played in groups of four, as well as in larger groups. It can also be played as a side game.

Quota Point

With *Quota Point*, all players take their handicap—beware of sandbaggers—and use that as their starting point for the game.

The points are based as follows:

- ❖ An eagle is worth 8 points
- ❖ A birdie is worth 4 points
- ❖ A par is worth 2 points
- ❖ A bogey is worth 1 point
- ❖ A double-bogey or higher is worth 0 points

The *Quota Point* game could be the easiest and fairest game for an entire group to play, no matter the skill level. For struggling golfers, it often takes only a hole or two to turn the tide, so it's a great way to keep everyone involved.

At the end of the game, take the points won and add them to your handicap. This can also be done at the completion of the front nine to give the group a running total at the turn. From that point you simply add the points on from there.

A modification to the handicap usage can be to,

instead of using full handicaps in the point total, work off the lowest handicap.

For example, if Player A is a 1-handicap, Player B is a 3-handicap, Player C is a 12-handicap, and Player D is an 18-handicap, the starting points would be the following: Player A has 0 points, Player B has 2 points, Player C has 11 points, and Player D has 17 points.

The winner gets the predetermined pot of money, or the losers simply hand over a brand new Taylor Made Tour Preferred golf ball or Titleist ProV1. Either way, given the price of golf balls these days, grown men do squirm just as much when having to hand over a brand new ball.

Total up the points at the end of the round, and you have yourself a winner.

Quota Point is also great game to play in groups of four players, as well as in larger groups.

Let it Ride

Let it Ride is a great game for the gamblers in the group.

Here's how *Let it Ride* works . . .

Depending on the level of golfers' skill in your group the *point base* is typically set at a bogey, and points are allotted as follows:

- ❖ 5 points for a bogey
- ❖ 15 points for a par
- ❖ 30 points for a birdie
- ❖ 60 points for an eagle

After winning points, each golfer has the choice of either banking their points or letting their points ride. If a player chooses to *let it ride*, all points they receive in the upcoming holes are doubled until they are banked.

Here's the kicker . . .

If a player chooses to *let it ride* and then goes on to make double-bogey or worse, they lose all the points they *let it ride* with, meaning the points not banked for that stretch.

At the end of the round, the players with the highest point totals are paid accordingly. The value per point is predetermined at the beginning of each round.

If you're a bit of a gambler, or simply have some streakiness to your game, then *Let it Ride* is certainly for you.

Let it Ride is also a great game for groups of four.

N.O.S.E.

When playing *N.O.S.E.*, golfers only count the scores of holes that begin with those letters. So in a full round of golf, the scores counted for each golfer will be on holes one, six, seven, eight, nine, eleven, sixteen, seventeen, and eighteen.

The remaining holes and their scores are tossed aside.

The same can be done for a quick 9-holes, where holes one, six, seven, eight, and nine are the only scores counted.

Back to the full round . . .

As a tiebreaker, simply use the number of putts on the N.O.S.E. holes. If still tied, consider awarding the tiebreaker to the player that hit the green in regulation and/or closest to the hole in regulation.

This game works for all playing abilities, however, if there is a difference within your group, you can use the handicap system on the N.O.S.E. holes and take the net scores.

N.O.S.E. is also a great game for groups of four golfers, as well as larger groups. You can also play *N.O.S.E.* as a side game.

Mulligans

Mulligans, as we all know, is a golf term for replaying a shot that we don't like.

Now, wouldn't you know it . . . Someone had to take it one step further and make a game of it!

Here's how *Mulligans* works . . .

A golfer gets to take a mulligan in a round of golf, up to the number of their handicap. If they are an 18-handicap, they get to replay up to 18 shots in that round of golf.

Obviously, the replayed shots are counted towards the score.

A note, however, would be to make sure you keep the pace of play, and to only play *Mulligans* if the entire group is in carts. No point in running all over the map searching for your sprayed shots.

Furthermore, if you or your group are set in a special, painstakingly long routine for each and every shot—as taught on The Golf Channel and Golf Digest—this game may not be for you, unless your idea of fun is a 6.5 hour round of golf!

Essentially, when deciding on *Mulligans*, always pay close attention to how busy the course is looking before starting so you are not disrupting pace of play.

Mulligans can be played with two, three, or four players, as well as in larger groups.

Pick Up Sticks

Pick Up Sticks is played in Match Play format, and can be played in competition of twosomes, threesomes, or two-man partners.

For the entirety of this chapter, let's assume that the *loser* on each hole is referred to as the other golfer or other two players or the other two-man team.

Here's how *Pick Up Sticks* plays out . . .

When Player A wins a hole, he selects a club of the losing opponent(s) to take out of play. Keep in mind, before the round starts, decide whether or not to grant the putter immunity. More skilled players can easily find a way to putt with any club in the bag, however, not the case with lesser skilled golfers.

Back to the game . . .

Player A selects a club from their opponent to take out of play. Typically, you may want to consider taking out the sand wedge first, as it is the most used club inside of 100-yards for golfers. Of course, it could be any club that you choose, based on your opponent's strengths or weaknesses. The cycle continues on each hole that is won.

The player can get a club back, in any order they

choose, when they win a hole.

Where there are three players in the group, if two players tie for the lowest score, they select a club to take out of the player with the highest score in the group.

The purpose of *Pick Up Sticks* is to put some fun and shot-making creativity back into your game. If you're all about scores and always having to enter a score into the computer for your handicap, *Pick Up Sticks* may not be for you.

Obvious question is how to make *Pick Up Sticks* work for use of handicaps?

The suggested method is to throw away the idea of stroke handicaps, and instead use the following:

- ✓ The higher-handicapped player removes one club from opponent's bag for every two strokes difference in their handicap.
- ✓ If Player A is an 8-handicap and Player B is a 14-handicap, Player B can remove three clubs from Player A's bag (14-8=6/2=3 clubs).

The game progresses as per usual, with clubs coming in and out of play as holes are won and lost.

Chicago

In *Chicago*, players receive a negative quota point, called a *hurdle*, which is based on their handicaps.

Chicago point system starts as follows . . .

Scratch players start with -39 points, a one-handicap starts at -38 points, a three-handicap starts at -36 points, and so on. A 36-handicap player (God help him!) starts with -3 points.

The allocation of points is as follows:

- ❖ A bogey is worth 1 point
- ❖ A par is worth 2 points
- ❖ A birdie is worth 4 points
- ❖ An eagle is worth 8 points
- ❖ An albatross (double-eagle) is worth 16 points

The winner is the golfer that clears their *hurdle* by the largest margin, whether in the plus or minus.

Have a predetermined wager set at the beginning of the round, that is paid to the winner or based on a point differential. Depending on how generous you are feeling, you can incorporate a bonus for the other players—the *losers* of the group—that still exceeded their individual hurdles.

Chicago can also be played in groups of four players, as well as in larger groups.

Auto Win

Auto Win works well with groups of two, three or four players.

The premise behind *Auto Win* is that a golfer automatically wins a hole when he accomplishes one of the following:

- ✓ Chip-in from off the green (chipping in from the fringe does not count).
- ✓ A hole-out from a sand bunker (or waste bunker).
- ✓ Stuffs an approach shot from 150-yards or more, or on par-3's (determine what constitutes *stuffing an approach shot*, in terms of distance from the flag—within a standard 35" putter length, for example—for your group).

If more than one player accomplishes an auto win on a hole you can either halve the points, no points rewarded, or a carry-over for the next auto win hole.

The player at the end of the round with the most points wins the game, and the cash that goes along with it.

If no holes are won in *Auto Win*, then there is nothing to carry over.

With *Auto Win*, you can either make it the betting game within your group or you can make it a game-within-a-game as a side bet.

Again, *Auto Win* can also be played with two or four players.

Red, White, Blue

In *Red, White, Blue*, all players begin the round by teeing off from the white tees (men's tees). Of course, tee block colors likely vary from course to course, but the premise is blue (back tees), white (men's tees) and red (ladies tees).

With each player teeing off on the first hole from the white tees, following the completion of the hole, players that make birdie now tee off on the next hole from the blue tees (back tees), the players that par stay on the white tees, and bogey or worse, well . . . hike up your skirt, Princess and tee it up from the ladies tee (red tees).

The process continues throughout the entire round, totaling up the score at the end to settle any predetermined wagers. Introducing the handicap system and taking net scores also works. Playing without the handicap system will have higher-handicap players playing from the red tees more often, but hey, maybe that's where they belong anyway!

Red, White, Blue is ideal for players with comparable skill levels (also with four players and larger groups).

Other Golf Games for 3 Players

The following games and their descriptions can be found in *Section 1, Golf Games for 2 Players*. These games are also ideal for groups of 3 players:

- ❖ Bisque — page 1
- ❖ Three Little Pigs — page 3
- ❖ Three Blind Mice — page 4
- ❖ Snake — page 5
- ❖ Mutt and Jeff — page 7
- ❖ Nassau — page 8

The following game and its description can be found in *Section 3, Golf Games for 4 Players*. This game is also ideal for groups of 3 players:

- ❖ Wolf — page 43

The following game and its description can be found in *Section 4, Golf Games for Larger Groups*. This game is also ideal for groups of 3 players:

- ❖ Ringer — page 77

SECTION 3

Golf Games for 4 Players

Wolf

Wolf is best played with four players, however, the game can be modified for three players.

Here's how Wolf works . . .

In *Wolf*, the rotational order for tee shots on each hole is determined before the round begins. The Wolf is the first player to tee off on every hole. If on the first hole Player A tees off first, followed by Player B, Player C, etc., then Player B tees off first on the second hole.

The games is as follows:

- ✓ Player A tees off, does not elect to go alone.
- ✓ Player B tees off, blows it dead right, hitting a house out-of-bounds; clearly Player A does not select Player B.
- ✓ Player C pipes one down the middle, Player A is impressed, therefore, partners with Player C.

Conversely, if the Wolf isn't impressed with any tee shots he witnesses, then he can play the hole alone—declaring solitary before leaving the tee box.

In a group of four players, holes #17 and #18 will not fall into the rotation. A courtesy would be to give the player(s) most in-debt from the round the opportunity to be the Wolf on those holes. If all players are equal in-debt (or winnings) simply continue with the rotation.

The allocation of points for *Wolf* is as follows:

- ✓ If the Wolf chooses a partner, and they beat the other team, the Wolf and his partner receive 2 points each.
- ✓ If the non-Wolf partners win the hole, they receive 3 points each.
- ✓ If the Wolf beats the group of three players, the Wolf gets 4 points.
- ✓ If the Wolf is beaten—has a higher score than the other three players—the winning group of three gets 1 point each.

A variation to *Wolf* is *Lone Wolf*, where the Wolf declares immediately after their tee shot they will play the hole alone. In this case, points are tripled—for wins and losses. One step further . . . If the Wolf declares he is going alone before the peg is in the ground or the ball is airborne, then all bets are quadrupled.

At the end of the round, grab a cold beverage, go over the points and start dishing out the cash.

Alternate Shot (aka Foursomes)

Alternate Shot has been made famous by the Ryder Cup, and its format is rather simple. However, for maximum enjoyment, consider playing when you have a few rounds under your belt . . . Especially if on a golf trip.

Before each round, you and your partner determine the rotational order of tee shots on each hole. For example, does Player A tee off on all odd-numbered holes or all even-numbered holes?

Once the decision has been made, *Alternate Shot* format has the partner that does not hit the tee shot hitting the second shot.

The team alternates until the ball is in the hole.

You can play either stroke play or match play, however, to get full appreciation of what those guys playing in the Ryder Cup experience, why not make it match play?

Some strategies when trying to determine which player tees off on what holes, it is best to grab a scorecard to look for as many nuances as possible.

For example, if you have a solid iron player as a partner, and the par-3's happen to fall all on odd-numbered holes, or rather consistently, then select that player to be the odd-numbered hole tee shot dude. This decision allows them to play to their strengths. Similarly, if you have a bomber off the tee as a partner, check out where the par-5's or long par 4's fall into place. If these holes are consistently even or odd-numbered holes, then base your decision on that.

Of course, golf is difficult and complicated enough at times, so no need to become a mental midget in the process. Simplify it, and whoever is ready to hit on the first hole first is the odd-numbered tee shot guy.

Perhaps take a page out of the European Ryder Cup Team as of late—they dominate the U.S. Ryder Cup Team in Alternate Shot—and just go out and play. Don't put too much thought into it.

Alternate Shot is also a great game for larger groups, obviously, as long as you have even-numbered players. If playing in larger groups, you can consider stroke play, however, playing a Ryder Cup format with match play is ideal.

Two-Man Best Ball (aka Four-Ball)

Two-Man Best Ball is also one of the formats we see played at the Ryder Cup.

A *Two-Man Best Ball* is when you have a group of four players partnered into teams of two.

There is no real special strategy when playing in this format, with the exception of which of the two players on the team hits first off the tee. The rule of thumb, typically, is to get a ball in play. If this is the goal, then the straighter and more consistent driver of the ball should tee off first. Once that is achieved, the longer hitter in the group can launch away to shorten the distance and put themselves in position, with a shorter club in hand to optimize the opportunity.

Order of play for a *Two-Man Best Ball* is similar to regular play in the sense that the player further from the green hits first. However, in a *Two-Man Best Ball* team format, if your partner is further from the hole, and you are much closer, you can in fact play first.

For example:

✓ Team A, Player A is on the green 28-feet from

the hole while Player B is on the green 7-feet from the hole.

✓ Team B, Player A is on the green 12-feet from the hole, while Player B is 10-feet from the hole.

✓ Team A has the honor on the green, however, if they so desire, Player B can roll their putt first.

When it comes to a *Two-Man Best Ball*, you are playing your own ball, so nothing overly-complicated about it. Take the best score from each team, lowest wins the hole (assuming match play format).

Two-Man Best Ball can be played straight up with no handicaps. Introduce the handicap system when playing in a group with varying skill levels. It will even the playing field.

The team that can *ham and egg* the best in *Two-Man Best Ball* normally comes out on top.

As with *Alternate Shot*, *Two-Man Best Ball* can be played in larger groups, as long as there are even-numbered players. If playing in larger groups, you can consider stroke play, however, playing a Ryder Cup format with match play is ideal.

Two-Man Scramble

Whether you are on a golf trip or playing your regular Saturday morning round at the club, a *Two-Man Scramble* is a great way to change things up.

Here's how a *Two-Man Scramble* plays . . .

Each player tees off on every hole, followed by each of the two golfers in the team determining which tee shot they want to hit their next shot from. This decision is normally based on positioning or the shortest length for the second shot. For par-3's, it's the closest to the hole or *easiest putt*. Once the group has selected the shot they would like to play from, follow that process until the ball is in the hole.

The strategy for a *Two-Man Scramble* normally involves the following:

✓ The more consistent driver of the ball hits the tee shot first, helping the team get a ball in play, while the longer hitter of the team hits second to shorten the distance to the hole—and swing out of their shoes if they have a ball in play.

✓ Another option is for the player that handles their nerves best to hit second, even if they may be the shorter of the two.

For ultimate enjoyment, a *Two-Man Scramble* is played in stroke play. See how low you can go.

Keep in mind, the terms *scramble* and *best-ball* are often confused amongst many golfers. A *scramble* is played as outlined above, whereas a *best-ball* format is the best score from a team, aka *Two-Man Best Ball, Four-Ball* (referring to a group of four golfers, partnered as two players). *See page 47.*

When playing a *Two-Man Scramble*, you may consider introducing handicaps to level the playing field if you have a wide range of skill levels. A *Two-Man Scramble* can also be played with larger groups with even-numbered players.

Two-Man Shamble

A *Two-Man Shamble* follows the same rules as a *Two-Man Scramble*, with one exception.

Here's how it looks . . .

Both players from each team hit tee shots just as in a *Two-Man Scramble*. In a *Two-Man Shamble*, they select the best positioned ball from the two tee shots, however, they now play their own ball from that point until they each hole out.

The best score from the two counts towards their team score.

Two-Man Shamble can also be played in large groups, with even-numbered players.

Vegas

Warning! Not for the faint of heart, likely why it wasn't named *Buttercup*!

Vegas requires a group of four players, paired into teams of two.

Here's the gist of what *Vegas* is all about . . .

You play each hole as you normally would, then at the end of each hole the scores are *paired* to make a total number. For example, if Player A makes a 3 and Player B makes a 5, the paired number is *35*. You keep track of the paired numbers for each hole on the scorecard, then at the completion of the round you simply determine the differential. This differential is how the bet is settled.

Of course, you can determine the differential after each hole to make tracking easier.

There is an important caveat to *Vegas* . . .

The cap for a score by a player is 9, meaning that if Player A makes a 3 and Player B makes a 10, the paired number is NOT *310* but instead *103*. It helps to keep things a little more reasonable.

Vegas is great for players of equal playing ability, but you can also apply the handicap system whereby the paired numbers are based on the handicap holes.

For example, you are playing the 8th hole, which according to the scorecard is the seventh most difficult hole on the course, Player A (a scratch golfer) scores a 3 and Player B (a 12-handicap) scores a 7, Player B's score would be a 6. The paired score for that hole would be *36*.

As the name *Vegas* states, this can be for *high rollers*. You can play for whatever dollar per point amount you prefer. If you really want to feel your palms sweat, play for a $2 per point. If you want to make it a little saner, a nickel or dime per point is your best option.

Once everyone is done battlin' it out on the golf course, tally up the points and start emptying your wallets for the winners.

Round Robin

Round Robin is a game for groups of four golfers, split into rotating teams of two.

Here's how *Round Robin* plays . . .

Three 6-hole matches are played, teams of two playing against another team of two. But here's where it gets interesting . . .

Players change partners after each 6-hole match so that each player in the foursome plays with every other player. This can be good or bad, depends on how you look at it.

The game *Round Robin* proceeds as follows:

- ❖ Holes 1 to 6, Player A and Player B partner to compete against Players C and D
- ❖ Holes 7 to 12, Player A and Player C partner to compete against Players B and D
- ❖ Holes 13 to 18, Player A and Player D partner to compete against Players B and C

Each 6-hole match represents a separate wager, therefore, your goal is to be on the winning side in at least two of the three matches.

As with all games, you set a predetermined wager prior to the round and use a point system per each round robin. At the completion of the round, settle the wager up over a couple of cold beverages in the clubhouse.

When playing *Round Robin*, it is best to be played by a group of equal playing abilities or using full handicaps. Also, you can use any playing format—*Two-Man Best Ball*, *Alternate Shot*, *Two-Man Scramble*, *Two-Man Shamble*, etc.

A similar game to *Round Robin* is *3 In 1*, which you can read about in the following chapter.

3 In 1

3 In 1 is a golf team competition format that works similar to *Round Robin*, and is also played in groups of four golfers, two against two.

With *3 In 1* you use three different scoring formats in one round of golf, with the format changing every six holes. Typically, it is best to play with better-known formats when playing *3 In 1*, so everyone in the group can focus on the game and not worry about anything else.

For example:

- ❖ Holes 1 to 6, play *Two-Man Best Ball*
- ❖ Holes 7 to 12, play *Alternate Shot*
- ❖ Holes 13 to 18, play *Two-Man Scramble* (or *Two-Man Shamble*)

As you can see, when playing *3 In 1*, you play with the same partner throughout the entire round.

Select stroke play or match play for scoring.

3 In 1 is also ideal when playing in larger groups that are even-numbered.

Irish Four Ball

Irish Four Ball uses the *Modified Stableford* scoring system, which is used at the PGA Tour's Barracuda in Renoe, Tahoe.

Irish Four Ball is for teams of four golfers, which is ideal for larger groups competing against each other.

There are three versions for *Irish Four Ball*, but first a look at how the point system looks, using the *Modified Stableford* scoring system:

- ❖ An eagle is worth 8 points
- ❖ A birdie is worth 5 points
- ❖ A par is worth 0 points
- ❖ A bogey is -1 points
- ❖ A double-bogey or worse is -3 points

Of course, this game is perfect for players of higher skill level, but as with most games, you can apply the handicap system and use net scores.

Here are the three versions:

Version 1 (Most Common)

Typically, in this version of *Irish Four Ball*, you take the two best scores per hole, therefore, the point calculation is based on the two best points. If, in the team, Player A gets 0 points, Player B gets 1 point, Player C gets -1 point, and Player D gets -3 points, the two best scores would total 1 point (0 plus 1).

The teams total the points at the end of the round, and the team with the highest score wins, which in this case, bragging about being +15 for the round is a good thing.

Version 2

The scoring system stays the same, however, the scores you use are different, as outlined here:

❖ Holes 1 thru 6 — one low ball score
❖ Holes 7 thru 11 — two low ball scores
❖ Holes 12 thru 15 — three low ball scores
❖ Holes 16 thru 18 — four low ball scores

Version 3

In this version, the point allocation remains, however, the points are based on *par* for the holes, as follows:

❖ Par 3's — two low ball scores
❖ Par 4's — three low ball scores
❖ Par-5's — four low ball scores

These are for four-man teams, however, the holes and the point structure can easily be modified for three-man teams as well with a little use of your imagination in Version 2 and Version 3.

Version 2 Modified for Teams of 3:

❖ Holes 1 thru 6 — one low ball score
❖ Holes 7 thru 12 — two low ball scores
❖ Holes 8 thru 13 — three low ball scores

Version 3 Modified for Teams of 3:

❖ Par-3's — one low ball score
❖ Par-4's — two low ball scores
❖ Par-5's — three low ball scores

To play *Irish Four Ball* in a competition format you will want to have a group of 8 players, 12 players, or 16 players, etc.

If you would like to modify Version 2 and Version 3 so you play in teams of three players, you will want to have groups of 6 players, 9 players, 12 players, etc.

Scotch Foursome

Scotch Foursome is a combo of a *Scramble* and *Alternate Shot*. It is played with teams of two, so ideal if you have a group of four, or a large group of even-number players to split into teams of two.

Here's how it works:

- ✓ Player A and Player B tee off on each hole.
- ✓ As a team, they select the ball they would like to play their second shot from.
- ✓ If Player A's ball is selected, then Player B plays the second shot.
- ✓ Continue with alternate shot until the ball is in the hole.

Scotch Foursome works well with players of equal ability, and can also be effectively used with handicaps for net score.

Alternate Shot (Scotch Foursome)

This format is a little different than the traditional *Alternate Shot* we watch during the Ryder Cup.

In *Alternate Shot Scotch Foursome*, teams of two, each player alternates on EVERY shot—meaning the following—assuming a Par-4 in this example:

- ✓ Player A tees off on hole #1.
- ✓ Player B hits the approach shot to 5-feet.
- ✓ Player A putts, has an *explosion* go off in their hands, leaving Player B with a 5-foot putt coming back.
- ✓ Player B in disbelief, takes a deep breath and casually rolls in the 5-footer for par.
- ✓ On hole #2, Player A tees off again, and the cycle continues.

Alternate Ball Scotch Foursome can also be played in larger groups of even-numbered players.

Gruesomes

Gruesomes is a modified format of *Alternate Shot* and *Scotch Foursome*, where both players tee off on the hole, however, there is a bit of a twist, as follows:

- ❖ Team A—both players tee off
- ❖ Team B selects where Team A plays from
- ❖ Team B—both players tee off
- ❖ Team A selects where Team B plays from

When choosing the other teams ball to play from, obviously, the idea is to select the worst of the two drives . . . the *gruesome* drive.

Now, if Team B selects the drive of Player A from Team A, then the second shot is also played by Player A. Following the second shot, alternate shot then ensues until the ball is in the hole.

Gruesomes is ideal for groups of four golfers with equal playing ability, however, handicaps and net score does work.

Bridge

Bridge is a great game for four golfers split into teams of two.

On the first tee, Team A determines the total score that they are going to complete the hole in, using the agreed upon gross or net scores from handicap.

Let's take a look at an example . . .

Team A determines that they will complete the hole in 10 strokes, and Team B has the three following options:

- ❖ Bid lower than 10
- ❖ Take the bet
- ❖ Take the bet and double it

If they so desire, Team A may double the bet back.

Once the bidding on the hole finishes, play the hole out and total the score up. You may choose to add a penalty point or dollar amount for each stroke the winning bidder incurs over a bogey.

Low Ball – High Ball

Low Ball – High Ball is ideal for groups of four, split into teams of two.

The premise behind the game is as follows:

- ✓ Team A—Player A makes a 4 and Player B makes a 6.
- ✓ Team B—Player A makes a 5 and Player B makes a 5.
- ✓ Team A wins a point for low score of 4 (compared to Team B's low score of 5), while Team B wins a point for the *lower* high score of 5 (compared to Team A's high score of 6).

Follow this process on each hole, and at the end of the round total up the points. The wager is paid to the winning team based on the predetermined dollar amount per hole.

If both sides tie for the low ball score, then the point can go unrewarded or it can carry over to the next hole, making it double the points.

You can also introduce extra points or double points for any scores that are birdies or eagles.

For example, par is 4 and a score of birdie 3. The team would get 2 points instead of 1 point for this score.

Other Golf Games for 4 Players

The following games and their descriptions can be found in *Section 1, Golf Games for 2 Players*. These games are also ideal for groups of 4 players:

The following games and their descriptions can be found in *Section 2, Golf Games for 3 Players*. These games are also ideal for groups of 4 players:

❖ Pick Up Sticks — page 32
❖ Chicago — page 34
❖ Auto Win — page 36
❖ Red, White, Blue — page 38

The following game and its description can be found in *Section 4, Golf Games for Larger Groups.* This game is also ideal for groups of 4 players:

❖ Ringer — page 77

SECTION 4

Golf Games for Larger Groups

Scramble

A *Scramble* is a very common game, often confused by golfers as *Best Ball*.

A *Scramble* is typically played as a four-man team.

In a *Scramble*, each player hits off the tee, followed by the group selecting the best positioned tee shot. From there, they each hit the next shot, then selecting the best positioned ball again.

Follow the process until the ball is in the hole.

A *Scramble* is ideal for larger groups of 8 players, 12 players, etc.

Scoring for a *Scramble* is most enjoyable in stroke play.

A *Scramble* can also be played in teams of three players, with larger groups of 6 players, 9 players, 12 players, etc.

Shamble

Shamble is a modified version of playing a *Scramble*.

In a *Shamble*, each player hits off the tee, the group also selects the best positioned ball for their next shot, however, instead of playing one ball until the ball is in the hole, they play their own ball from that position.

The scoring can be the best score from that group, or, instead, it can be the total of the two lowest scores.

You may want to consider other scoring variations to change it up, whereby you take the total of the lowest and the highest score, keeping everyone involved.

Tally up the scores at the end of the round, and settle the wagers over a cold beverage or two.

Similar to a *Scramble*, a *Shamble* is ideal for larger groups wanting to have a competition amongst themselves.

A *Shamble* can also be played in teams of three players.

Bowmaker

Bowmaker is a good game if you have a group of six players or eight players, or more.

For this example, if you have a group of eight players you divide the group into teams of four. At the beginning of the round you set a predetermined wager to be paid out at the end of the round.

In *Bowmaker*, each golfer plays their own golf ball in stroke play format. At the end of each hole you take the totals of the best two scores (or three to really make it interesting). Upon completion of the round, total up the scores.

For example, hole #1:

- ❖ Player A makes a 3
- ❖ Player B makes a 4
- ❖ Player C makes a 6
- ❖ Player D makes a 7

In this example, the scores for the group would be as follows:

If we go on the premise that the two best scores are taken, the total for the first hole is 7 (3 plus 4). If we go on the premise that the three lowest scores are taken, the total for the first hole is 13 (3 plus 4 plus 6).

Bowmaker is ideal for players of equal playing abilities, and of course, can be used with handicaps taking the net scores and adding them up for your total.

Whack 'N' Hack

Whack 'N' Hack is a game for teams of four, so very good for larger groups.

Here's how *Whack 'N' Hack* starts . . .

Each player plays their own ball in stroke play format. At the end of each hole, the team takes their lowest score and their highest score, adding them up for the team total, which would look as follows:

- ❖ Player A scores a 4
- ❖ Player B scores a 5
- ❖ Player C scores a 5
- ❖ Player D scores a 7

The team score for this hole would be 11, the sum total of the lowest score of 4 and the highest score of 7.

There is a catch to *Whack 'N' Hack* . . .

If the team's lowest score is a birdie, then that team totals their two lowest scores for the team total.

This game is good for players of equal skill level and for playing with handicaps, going off of net scores.

4-Man Cha Cha Cha

4-Man Cha Cha Cha is also known as *1-2-3 Best Ball*.

4-Man Cha Cha Cha is ideal for larger groups, splitting the teams into groups of four.

In *4-Man Cha Cha Cha* there is a rotation of scores that are counted for the team, which makes it ideal to keep all players involved. This can be seen in the following:

- ✓ On the first hole, the lowest score of the group is taken.
- ✓ On the second hole, the totals of the two lowest scores in the group are taken.
- ✓ On the third hole, the totals of the lowest three scores in the group are taken.
- ✓ On the fourth hole, the process starts over with the lowest score of the group, and continues through each hole as outlined above.

4-Man Cha Cha Cha is ideal for players of equal skill levels, and of course, using handicaps as well.

Ringer

Ringer is ideal for a golf trip with several players, played over two or more rounds at the same golf course. Of course, you can play *Ringer* when playing two or more rounds at several golf courses. For the course you play only once you can include the score for your tournament total as well.

But first, let's go through the format for *Ringer* . . .

The scores are kept with stroke play scoring. At the end of the week of golf, each golfer takes the best scores from each hole played, essentially giving them a new 18-hole score for that one particular golf course played. If other courses are played more than once, simply repeat the process for that course as well.

Here is how it looks:

- ✓ During the first round, Player X scores a 3, 4, and 3 on holes 1, 2, and 3.
- ✓ During the second round at the same course, Player X scores a 4, 3, and 2 on holes 1, 2, and 3.
- ✓ During the third round at the same course, Player X scores a 6, 5, and a 1 on holes 1, 2, and

3.

- ✓ The scores they would take are 3, 3, and 1 for holes #1, 2, and 3.
- ✓ Continue the process for the entire scorecard and for other courses you play multiple times.
- ✓ Total the best 18 scores for each course for your tournament or week total.

Again, if you happen to play a course only once, then you can take that score and add to your best 18 scores from each course for your weekly total as well.

Ringer is ideal for players of equal abilities, as well as using handicaps for net scoring.

Ringer can also be played in groups of three or four players.

Other Golf Games for Larger Groups

The following games and their descriptions can be found in *Section 1, Golf Games for 2 Players*. These games are also ideal for larger groups of players:

- ❖ Bisque — page 1
- ❖ Three Little Pigs — page 3
- ❖ Three Blind Mice — page 4
- ❖ Mutt and Jeff — page 7

The following games and their descriptions can be found in *Section 2, Golf Games for 3 Players*. These games are also ideal for larger groups of players:

- ❖ Skins — page 23
- ❖ Quota Points — page 25
- ❖ N.O.S.E. — page 29
- ❖ Mulligans — page 30
- ❖ Chicago — page 34
- ❖ Red, White, Blue — page 38

The following games and their descriptions can be

found in *Section 3, Golf Games for 4 Players*. These games are also ideal for larger groups of players:

SECTION 5

Side Games

Favorite Holes

Favorite Holes is a side-bet for a game within a game, and works especially well if you are familiar with a course and have favorite holes that you normally do well on. It can also be used on golf trips, basing it on your bias towards par-3's or par-5's or loving the idea of short par-4's.

Here's how *Favorite Holes* works:

- ✓ Agree on a predetermined wager prior to each round.
- ✓ Each golfer selects their three individual favorite holes prior to the round.
- ✓ At the end of the round, each player totals up their score for those three holes.
- ✓ The player with the lowest three hole total wins the pot for the side bet.

IMPORTANT:

When totaling up the three hole total, use the relative to par score not the total. This avoids any problems if a player selects par-3's as their favorites compared to a player that selects all par-5's as their favorites, therefore, whoever has the best score relative to par wins.

Favorite Holes can be played with gross scores and using handicaps for net scores.

Arnies

Arnies is named after Arnold Palmer for his aggressive style of play.

Here's how *Arnies* work . . .

A player that makes a par without ever being in the fairway gets a point.

At the end of the round, the group totals up the number of *Arnies*, and the wagers are paid up.

Arnies are only paid up on par-4's and par-5's.

Obviously, golfers do not set out to miss fairways as your intent is to play as good as possible but this game brings in an added element of fun, and rewards players for making pars out of tough spots.

This game is also known as *Seve*, named after the great Seve Ballesteros.

Bounce Back

Surely you have heard of the "Bounce Back" stats while watching a PGA tournament on television. Well, this game is very similar.

With *Bounce Back*, when a player makes a double-bogey or worse, they receive points when they follow that hole up with a par or better. The points are pre-determined by your group prior to the round of golf.

Of course, as much as you should be rewarded for bouncing back after a poor hole, you should equally feel the pain of back-to-back double-bogies. When this happens, a person loses one point.

Barkies

Barkies is a great side game, adding a little more fun into the round.

Here's how *Barkies* works . . .

When a player hits a tree on a hole—leaves don't count—and makes a par on that hole, it is considered a barkie. The value of the barkies are determined before the round starts.

One step further . . . If a player hits two trees on a hole, and somehow manages to scramble out a par, then the points are doubled.

And another step further . . . If a player hits a tree and makes a birdie on the hole, then the points are doubled.

The points in *Barkies* are tallied up and totaled for a small group or a larger group at the end of the round.

Sandies

Sandies is similar to *Barkies*, with the exception that a player gets a point when they have been in a bunker on a hole and make a par.

If a player holes out from a greenside bunker for birdie, you can triple the points. And if a player holes out from a greenside bunker for a par or higher, you can certainly be generous to make it double points. Your call.

Of course, we must also consider the possibility of a player holing their shot from a bunker for eagle. As this would be quite the feat, make it quadruple points.

Waste bunkers are not considered hazards—a player can ground their club in a waste bunker—but it does not make the shot any less difficult, so this would also be considered a sandie.

The point value is predetermined at the beginning of the round, typically set at $1 Sandies.

Sandies can be a side game for all group sizes.

Splashies

Splashies is another side game that rewards *bad play turned good*.

And it's quite simple:

A player wins a *Splashie* when they have hit their ball into the water, and still found a way to make a par.

As with the other games, you can take it one step further—likely seen on a par-5 hole out shot—and give triple points when a player plays hard for birdie after hitting their ball in the water.

Splashies can be a side game for all group sizes.

Other Side Games

The following games and their descriptions can be found in *Section 1, Golf Games for 2 Players*. These games are also ideal side games:

❖ Snake — page 5
❖ Mutt and Jeff — page 7

The following games and their descriptions can be found in *Section 2, Golf Games for 3 Players*. These games are also ideal side games:

❖ Bingo, Bango, Bongo! — page 17
❖ Skins — page 23
❖ N.O.S.E. — page 29
❖ Auto Win — page 36

Index of Golf Games

Use this index to navigate through *Golf Games* in search of the best game(s) for your group.

2 = 2 players in a group

3 = 3 players in a group

4 = 4 players in a group

+ = larger groups

side = games played on the side

	# of players
Favorite Holes (p.83)	side
Gruesomes (p.62)	4
Irish Four Ball (p.57)	4, +
Let it Ride (p.27)	3, 4
Low Ball – High Ball (p.64)	4
Mulligans (p.30)	2, 3, 4, +
Mutt and Jeff (p.7)	2, 3, 4, +, side
N.O.S.E. (p.29)	3, 4, +, side
Nassau (p.8)	2, 3, 4
Nine Points (p.19)	3
Pick Up Sticks (p.32)	2, 3, 4
Quota Point (p.25)	3, 4, +
Rabbit (p.21)	3, 4
Red, White, Blue (p.38)	3, 4, +
Ringer (p.77)	3, 4, +
Round Robin (p.54)	4
Sandies (p.88)	side
Scotch Foursome (p.60)	4, +
Scramble (p.71)	+
Shamble (p.72)	+
Skins (p.23)	3, 4, +, side
Snake (p.5)	2, 3, 4, side
Splashies (p.89)	side
Three Blind Mice (p.4)	2, 3, 4, +
Three Little Pigs (p.3)	2, 3, 4, +
Two-Man Best Ball (p.47)	4, +
Two-Man Scramble (p.49)	4, +
Two-Man Shamble (p.51)	4, +

ABOUT GOLF TRIP JUNKIE

Golf has been our passion for 30 years.

We have been very fortunate to play close to 200 golf courses around the world, which includes a highly memorable 12-day, 18-round of golf experience in Scotland. We also drove approximately 1,500 miles to play those courses, but, admittedly, that's just plain foolish . . . Fun, but foolish!

Some may even say ludicrous, ridiculous, stupid, and a tad bit on the crazy side.

However, during this *foolish* endeavor we aspired to live out our golfing dreams. Just like you, our dreams included playing and walking the hollow grounds of the historic Old Course at St. Andrews.

We're very proud and pleased to say we did, so we can knock cross that one off our list! (That's a lie . . . It's still on the list . . . To play again!).

Many golfers, including us, have had the unique pleasure of also experiencing first tee jitters at other historic courses in the British Open Rota—The Ailsa Course at Turnberry and The Honourable Company of Edinburgh Golfers (Muirfield)—very special places where greats of the game competed. Jack Nicklaus,

Tiger Woods, Nick Faldo, and Seve Ballesteros, just to name a few.

These experiences will not soon be forgotten!

Along the way we also discovered hidden gems in The Championship Course at Royal Dornoch and North Berwick West Links, which to this day, both stand as favorites for Golf Trip Junkie.

That's our Scotland experience, in a nutshell.

Now to the U.S. of A . . .

At Golf Trip Junkie we have also been very fortunate to play many rewarding golf courses in the deserts of Arizona, Nevada, and California. If you've never been or haven't played enough of them, you are most definitely in for an amazing treat! Far too many courses that we have played to list, but waiting for you are gems such as Golfweeks #1 ranked course you can play in Arizona—We-Ko-Pa's Saguaro Course—a Coore and Crenshaw masterpiece! Hint: You definitely want to add We-Ko-Pa (both courses) to your list of *must play*.

Of course, we cannot forget the golf meccas of the Carolina's and Florida. As with many of the other states in the U.S., there are just too many great courses to list, but personal favorites are Pinehurst Resort, Tobacco Road, and Pine Needles in North Carolina, Kiawah Island Resort and Sea Pines Resort in South Carolina, and Southern Pines, Orange County National, and Pine Barrens at World Woods Resort in Florida.

All of these wonderful golf experiences (and plenty of others) were planned in great detail and went off without a hitch.

At Golf Trip Junkie, we multiply the detail put into every trip to ensure everyone's experience exceeds our own.

That's our primary goal!

As golfers, we know that playing a round of golf with a clouded-mind filled with stressors does not result in a memorable experience. That's simply no fun!

We know what the stressors look like for most everyone, and the unnecessary frustration and aggravation when trying to plan a golf trip on your own—booking your courses to play, tee times, replay bookings, accommodations, and transportation.

Instead, leave it to us to fulfill your needs.

Golf Trip Junkie eliminates any of these concerns, allowing you to focus on what is most important in your trip . . . To have enough golf balls, ensure your clothes are color coordinated, and that your golf game is sharp and ready to go come the first tee shot on the first day.

Essentially, with Golf Trip Junkie's personal touch and custom golf packages all you have to do is show up . . . Loose, limber, focused, and ready for the extraordinary fun your golf trip will bring!

GTJ's SERVICES

At Golf Trip Junkie, we pride ourselves on serving golfers with precisely what they are looking for in a golf vacation.

Simple. Fun. Memorable. Stress free. And nothing less than awesome golf courses and accommodations!

We realize that golf fanatics come in all shapes and sizes. Some want to eat, sleep, drink, and breathe golf the entire time, while others enjoy the idea of different experiences sprinkled in each day.

No matter what level of golf fanatic you are, Golf Trip Junkie will make your trip work for you, from booking tee times (and replays), your accommodations, your transportation, activities for non-golf companions, dinner reservations (if you so desire), tours, and anything else you can think of. Our goal is to serve you, with whatever you are looking for—standard ready-made Stay & Play Golf Packages—or our specialty—Custom-Built Golf Vacations.

Here is just a small glimpse of what we do for our valued customers to ensure they receive maximum fun and exceptional value:

Custom-Built Golf Vacations: "Uber Awesome Golf Holidays."

Our primary focus is to create custom-built golf vacations for the traveling golfer and their companions. When booking your golf trip through Golf Trip Junkie you will have hundreds of golf courses and lodging options to choose from throughout the United States and Internationally. When we put pen-to-paper and do our thing, we are extremely confident that the final result will be precisely what you are looking for.

We believe that the best golf vacations are the ones that are individually tailored, however, the planning process often takes a great deal of time for busy folks, which is why golfers typically look for the standard ready-made packages. Our initiative is to gear our efforts to give you a perfectly personalized golf vacation package from the moment you leave to the moment you return home, and everything in between.

No matter what you are looking for in your next golf vacation, Golf Trip Junkie will be able to fulfill your needs and meet your requirements.

Premium Service Golf Packages

Our premium service options are something that we

are very excited about! The purpose of these options is to further maximize your enjoyment on your well-deserved golf holiday.

These premium options are broken down into two different packages—Private Driver and Private Jet packages. Pretty self-explanatory as these options provide you and your golf companions with a little something extra and special for you next golf vacation . . . Luxury travel at its finest!

The Buddy's Golf Trip

Golf Trip Junkie recognizes that some of the most memorable moments spent with your buddy's are on the golf course, in particular on golf vacations. They are memories that last a lifetime, so we ensure that everything runs as smoothly as possible so all you need to think about is your golf game, having some laughs with your closest friends, and winning all the bets (And side bets!) you possibly can.

Couple's Golf Trip

For you couples out there looking for a nice relaxing golf getaway, Golf Trip Junkie will provide you with everything you are looking for. We recognize that for some couples, trying to plan even the simplest of things—which movie to see on a Friday night—can be a daunting task. Planning and stress is often magnified when getting all the details right for a golf trip. Instead, let Golf Trip Junkie take care of all the details and remove any unnecessary stress by serving you with the ultimate golf vacation experience.

Ladies Golf Trip

At Golf Trip Junkie, serving the ladies with the ultimate golf trip oasis is one of our specialties. Not only do we take care of all your tee time needs, but we will also set up and point you in the right direction for your post-golf relaxation and fun.

We realize that for guys, their post-golf activities normally consist of beer and pizza, meanwhile the women golfers out there are the ones that truly have it figured out. Yes, you enjoy your cold beverage as well, but you also realize the value of being pampered with spa activities, from pedicures and manicures all the way through to a hot stone massage. Of course, we cannot forget about yoga as well. Tell us what you envision for your perfect oasis, and we'll make it happen.

Corporate Golf Travel

Golf Trip Junkie certainly recognizes the connection between the corporate world and the game of golf, as you pledge to treat your valued clients and staff with a special golf retreat.

Because the golf course is where long-standing,

strong business relationships are forged and deals are made, the magnitude will never be under-estimated by Golf Trip Junkie!

We value our corporate clients, and understand that you have a marketing budget, and behind that marketing budget are goals that are vital to future successes of your company. While putting together your corporate golf retreat, as with all golf trips we plan, there is no stone left unturned. No detail is too small!

Tours

Setting up tours—both golf and non-golf related—is an area of focus that we are very proud of!

Thanks to one of the biggest names in golf—Taylor Made Golf—Golf Trip Junkie has been given the green light to set up complimentary tours of their first class headquarters in Carlsbad, CA for our customers visiting the San Diego area.

With our European golf trips, we expand our services beyond golf, giving you a wider breadth of experience while venturing overseas. Our tour package offerings are second-to-none.

Car Rentals

We are pleased to announce that our preferred car rental agency is the Avis/Budget Car Rental Group. If you require a rental, simply let us know and we will get you rollin' on down the highway, with the top down and the music playin'.

Travel Insurance

We are also pleased to be teaming up with Travel Guard as we expand our product offerings. In a matter of minutes, Golf Trip Junkie can provide you with a travel insurance quote that will best protect you and your group.

Luggage Forward

We have traveled enough in our day to know that lugging around golf equipment is often not the most appealing proposition, therefore, we are pleased to offer Luggage Forward as an option for the traveling golfer. Essentially, once your golf vacation is booked, you ship your golf equipment out a few days before you are scheduled to leave, and they will be waiting for you upon your arrival at your golf destination.

GTJ's USA GOLF DESTINATIONS

The following are current United States golf destinations available for you when planning your next golf vacation. As we are continuously adding to our destinations, you can go to GOLFTRIPJUNKIE.COM to view our most recent up-to-date list.

- ❖ Scottsdale, AZ
- ❖ Tuscon, AZ
- ❖ Napa Valley, CA
- ❖ Palm Springs, CA
- ❖ Pebble Beach®, CA
- ❖ San Diego, CA
- ❖ Brooksville, FL
- ❖ Daytona Beach, FL
- ❖ Fort Lauderdale, FL
- ❖ Fort Myers, FL
- ❖ Jacksonville, FL
- ❖ Miami, FL
- ❖ Naples, Marco Island, FL
- ❖ Orlando, FL

- ❖ Palm Coast, FL
- ❖ Port St. Lucie, FL
- ❖ Sarasota, FL
- ❖ Space Coast, Cocoa Beach, FL
- ❖ St. Augustine, FL
- ❖ St. Petersburg, FL
- ❖ Tampa, FL
- ❖ West Palm Beach, FL
- ❖ Kohala Coast, Big Island, HI
- ❖ Gaylord, MI
- ❖ Biloxi, Gulfport, MS
- ❖ Las Vegas, NV
- ❖ Albuquerque, NM
- ❖ Pinehurst, NC
- ❖ Sandhills, NC
- ❖ Kiawah Island (Charleston), SC
- ❖ Hilton Head, SC
- ❖ Myrtle Beach, SC
- ❖ San Antonio, TX
- ❖ Kohler, WI (Whistling Straits)
- ❖ Williamsburg, VA

GTJ's INTERNATIONAL GOLF DESTINATIONS

The following are current International golf destinations available for you when planning your next golf vacation. As we are continuously adding to our destinations, you can go to GOLFTRIPJUNKIE.COM to view our most recent up-to-date list.

❖ Central Scotland
❖ The Highlands (Scotland)
❖ Edinburgh & East Lothian (Scotland)
❖ Aberdeen & Northeast Scotland
❖ St. Andrews, Fife & Carnoustie (Scotland)
❖ West Coast Scotland
❖ Dublin & The East (Ireland)
❖ Northern Ireland
❖ Southwest Ireland
❖ West & Northwest Ireland
❖ London, England
❖ Northwest London

- ❖ Southeast London
- ❖ Southwest London
- ❖ Portugal
- ❖ South Africa
- ❖ Spain
- ❖ North Wales
- ❖ South Wales
- ❖ Rio Grande, PR

WWW.GOLFTRIPJUNKIE.COM